We Love Holidays

EASTER

Saviour Pirotta

PowerKiDS
press.

New York

Saviour Pirotta is a highly experienced author, who has written many books for young children. He was born in Malta and is also a trained chef.

Published in 2008 by The Rosen Publishing Group, Inc.
29 East 21st Street, New York, NY 10010

First Edition

The publishers would like to thank the following for allowing us to reproduce their pictures in this book:

Corbis: cover, title page, 9, Ariel Skelley; 6, Albright-Knox Art Gallery; 7, Richard T. Nowitz; 8, Lucidio Studio Inc.; 11, Philip Gould; 12, Oswaldo Rivas; 15, Alinari Archives; 16, Clay Perry; 18 Craig Aurness; 23, Ronnie Kaufman / Alamy: 17, Oote Boe; 20, PhotoCuisine. / Robert Harding: 4, 13, 14, 22 / Getty Images: 19, Jutta Klee, Taxi; 21, Paul Webster, Stone / Wayland picture library: 5, 10

Library of Congress Cataloging-in-Publication Data

Pirotta, Saviour.
  Easter / Saviour Pirotta. -- 1st ed.
    p. cm. -- (We love holidays)
  Includes index.
  ISBN - 13: 978-1-4042-3705-6 (library binding)
  ISBN - 10: 1-4042-3705-4 (library binding)
  1. Easter--Juvenile literature. I. Title.
  BV55.P555 2007
  263'.93--dc22
                                                2006026792

Manufactured in China

Contents

Easter is here!

Happy Easter! Happy Easter! All over the world, many people celebrate Easter. For Christians, it is the biggest festival of the year.

In the Czech Republic, decorations are hung up in towns and cities. ▼

4

In some
countries,
children make
Easter cards
to send
to friends
and family. ▼

Easter can take place on
any Sunday between
March 22nd and
April 25th. However,
Christians start
preparing for
it long before.

Easter Miracle!

Artists such as Gauguin have painted Jesus's death on the cross.
▼

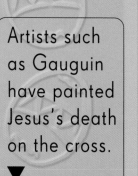

Easter is the happy ending to a sad story. The Christian leader **Jesus Christ** taught people how to love one another and God. Yet Jesus was put to death by men who did not understand him.

But Christians believe Jesus came back to life three days later.

When Jesus's friends visited his tomb, they found it empty. The tomb can still be seen in Israel today.
▼

7

New life

In countries of the Northern **Hemisphere**, Easter is in the springtime. Springtime is when the earth also comes back to life after the cold, dark days of winter.

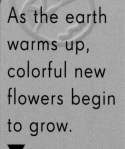

As the earth warms up, colorful new flowers begin to grow.
▼

New leaves appear on the trees.
Plants and flowers grow again.

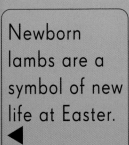

Newborn lambs are a symbol of new life at Easter. ◀

Preparing for Easter

Some people make **pancakes** the day before Lent. ▼

Christians start to prepare for Easter forty days before. This is a period called **Lent**. It starts on a special day called Ash Wednesday.

DID YOU KNOW?

People have their foreheads marked with ash to show they are sorry for their wrongdoings, or sins.

During Lent, many people give up treats, like candy or watching their favorite television program, to show how grateful they are for what Jesus did.

In the Caribbean, people have a carnival before Lent. They wear colorful costumes.
▼

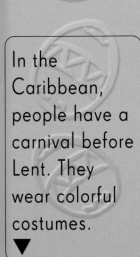

Holy Week

The last week of Lent is called Holy Week. It begins on Palm Sunday, a day when people welcomed Jesus as their king and laid **palm** branches at his feet.

In some churches, people are given a small cross, made of palm fronds. ▶

In many places, Christians carry palm branches and join the Palm Sunday **procession** in which a **statue** of Jesus is carried.

In parts ▲ of Africa, people carry decorated crosses through the streets.

13

Good Friday

Jesus died on the Friday before Easter, a day Christians call Good Friday. Good Friday is a very **solemn** day. Many churches are draped in black cloth, and there may be processions showing scenes of the last few hours of Jesus's life.

This painting shows Jesus sharing the last meal with his friends before his death on the cross.

DID YOU KNOW?

In church, the Good Friday service is based on the events leading up to Jesus's death on the cross.

Happy Easter!

The serious mood of Good Friday lasts until Saturday night, when Christians spend time thinking about what Jesus means to them. Then Easter Sunday is a happy day.

▲
On Easter Sunday, flowers fill the church with perfume.

DID YOU KNOW?

Many countries have a procession to celebrate Jesus's return.

Church bells ring to announce
that Jesus has come back to life.
Churches are filled with flowers.

Delicious eggs

Many children are given candy eggs and hard-boiled eggs. The egg is a symbol of Easter because a chick, a new life, comes out of it when it hatches. In the past, eggs were used to celebrate the springtime.

In the Ukraine, Easter eggs are decorated with beautiful patterns and colors. ▼

Hunting for Easter eggs is a popular game. ▼

Today, people in the United States and Eastern Europe still decorate real eggs with beautiful patterns.

19

Time for a feast

Lamb, the symbol of Jesus, is the most popular Easter meal in many countries. ▼

After giving up treats for Lent, people like to enjoy good food at Easter.

Easter treats vary around the world.
People in Greece have a special Easter
cheesecake. Italians munch a cake shaped
like a dove, called a colomba.

Let's celebrate!

In Mexico, people take to the streets to eat and drink. In France, children are told to watch for flying church bells, while their parents hide eggs in the yard for them to find.

Native Mexicans perform a traditional Easter dance.
▼

There are also **parades** in the streets.
Happy Easter! Happy Easter!

School children in Britain make Easter bonnets and dress up for an Easter parade. ◄

23

Index

Glossary

Ash the powder that is left when something has been burned

Jesus Christ the person who started the Christian religion

Lent the forty days before Easter, when Christians give up treats

Nazareth the place where Jesus Christ was born

hemisphere one half of the planet Earth, divided by a line called the equator

palm a tropical tree with fan-shaped leaves

pancake a flat cake made from flour, egg, and milk

parade a colorful procession in the streets

procession a group of people moving forward together

solemn when a person or event is serious

statue a crafted figure of a person or animal